Love Poems Of Herrick

THE LOVER'S LIBRARY

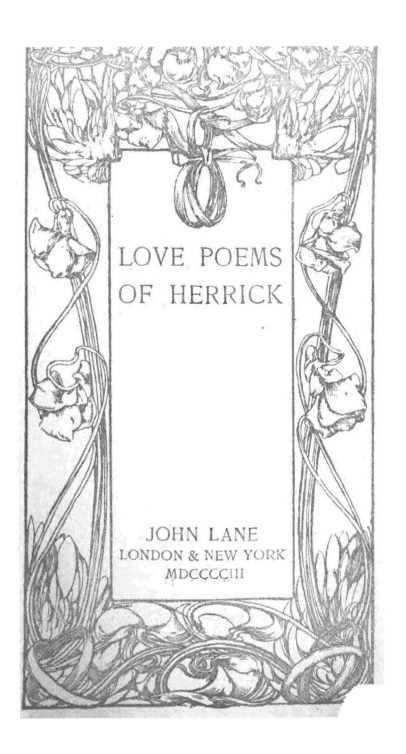

LOVE POEMS
OF HERRICK

JOHN LANE
LONDON & NEW YORK
MDCCCCIII

INDEX TO FIRST LINES

vi

INDEX TO FIRST LINES

viii

x

xi

UPON HIMSELF

THOU shalt not all die ; for, while
   love's fire shines
Upon his altar, men shall read thy
   lines,
And learn'd musicians shall, to honour
   Herrick's
Fame and his name, both set and sing
   his lyrics.

A   1

TO SILVIA TO WED

LET us, though late, at last, my
    Silvia, wed,
And loving lie in one devoted bed.
Thy watch may stand, my minutes fly
    post-haste ;
No sound calls back the year that
    once is past.
Then, sweetest Silvia, let's no longer
    stay ;
True love, we know, precipitates
    delay.
Away with doubts, all scruples hence
    remove ;
No man at one time can be wise and
    love.

2

THE PARLIAMENT OF ROSES TO JULIA

I DREAMT the roses one time went
 To meet and sit in parliament ;
The place for these, and for the rest
Of flowers, was thy spotless breast,
Over the which a state was drawn
Of tiffanie or cobweb lawn.
Then in that parly all those powers
Voted the rose the queen of flowers ;
But so as that herself should be
The maid of honour unto thee.

NO BASHFULNESS IN BEGGING

TO get thine ends, lay bashfulness
 aside ;
Who fears to ask doth teach to be
 deny'd.

3

TO PERENNA

WHEN I thy parts run o'er, I can't
espy
In any one the least indecency;
But every line and limb diffused thence
A fair and unfamiliar excellence:
So that the more I look the more I
prove
There's still more cause why I the
more should love.

THE WOUNDED HEART

COME bring your sampler, and
with art
Draw in't a wounded heart
And dropping here and there:
Not that I think that any dart

4

Can make yours bleed a tear,
    Or pierce it anywhere;
Yet do it to this end : that I
        May by
          This secret see,
    Though you can make
That heart to bleed, yours ne'er will
    ache
        For me.

NO LOATHSOMENESS
IN LOVE

WHAT I fancy I approve,
    No dislike there is in love:
Be my mistress short or tall,
And distorted therewithal :
Be she likewise one of those
That an acre hath of nose :
Be her forehead and her eyes
Full of incongruities :

5

Be her cheeks so shallow too
As to show her tongue wag through ;
Be her lips ill hung or set,
And her grinders black as jet :
Hath she thin hair, hath she none,
She's to me a paragon.

TO ANTHEA

IF, dear Anthea, my hard fate it be
    To live some few sad hours after
      thee,
Thy sacred corse with odours I will
    burn
And with my laurel crown thy golden
    urn.
Then holding up there such religious
    things
As were time past, thy holy filletings,

Near to thy reverend pitcher I will
    fall
Down dead for grief, and end my woes
    withal:
So three in one small plot of ground
    shall lie—
Anthea, Herrick, and his poetry.

THE WEEPING CHERRY

I SAW a cherry weep, and why?
    Why wept it? but for shame
Because my Julia's lip was by,
    And did out-red the same.
But, pretty fondling, let not fall
    A tear at all for that:
Which rubies, corals, scarlets, all
    For tincture wonder at.

LOVE, WHAT IT IS

LOVE is a circle that doth restless
    move
In the same sweet eternity of love.

PRESENCE AND ABSENCE

WHEN what is lov'd is present,
    love doth spring;
But being absent, love lies languishing.

THE POMANDER BRACELET

TO me my Julia lately sent
    A bracelet richly redolent:
The beads I kissed, but most lov'd her
That did perfume the pomander.

8

THE SHOE TYING

ANTHEA bade me tie her shoe;
  I did; and kissed the instep too:
And would have kissed unto her knee,
Had not her blush rebuked me.

THE CARCANET

INSTEAD of orient pearls of jet
  I sent my love a carcanet;
About her spotless neck she knit
The lace, to honour me or it:
Then think how rapt was I to see
My jet t'enthral such ivory.

HIS SAILING FROM JULIA

WHEN that day comes, whose
  evening says I'm gone
Unto that watery desolation,

9

Devoutly to thy closet-gods then pray
That my wing'd ship may meet no
    remora.
Those deities which circum-walk the
    seas,
And look upon our dreadful passages,
Will from all dangers re-deliver me
For one drink-offering poured out by
    thee.
Mercy and truth live with thee! and
    forbear
(In my short absence) to unsluice a
    tear ;
But yet for love's sake let thy lips do
    this,
Give my dead picture one engendering
    kiss :
Work that to life, and let me ever
    dwell
In thy remembrance, Julia.   So fare-
    well.

HOW THE WALL-FLOWER CAME FIRST, AND WHY SO CALLED

WHY this flower is now call'd so,
    List, sweet maids, and you
      shall know.
Understand this firstling was
Once a brisk and bonnie lass,
Kept as close as Danæ was:
Who a sprightly springall lov'd,
And to have it fully prov'd,
Up she got upon a wall,
Tempting down to slide withal:
But the silken twist untied,
So she fell, and, bruis'd, she died.
Love, in pity of the deed,
And her loving-luckless speed,
'Turn'd her to this plant we call
Now *the flower of the wall.*

11

WHY FLOWERS CHANGE COLOUR

THESE fresh beauties (we can prove)
Once were virgins sick of love,
Turn'd to flowers.   Still in some
Colours go and colours come.

TO HIS MISTRESS OB-JECTING TO HIM NEITHER TOYING OR TALKING

YOU say I love not, 'cause I do not play
Still with your curls, and kiss the time away.
You blame me too, because I can't devise

12

Some sport to please those babies in
　　your eyes:
By love's religion, I must here confess
　　it,
The most I love when I the least ex-
　　press it.
Small griefs find tongues: full casks
　　are ever found
To give (if any, yet) but little sound.
Deep waters noiseless are; and this
　　we know
That chiding streams betray small
　　depth below.
So, when love speechless is, she doth
　　express
A depth in love and that depth
　　bottomless.
Now, since my love is tongueless,
　　know me such
Who speak but little 'cause I love so
　　much

B　　　　　　　　　　　13

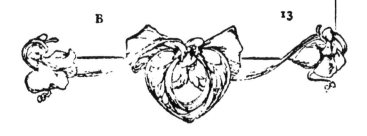

THE DREAM

METHOUGHT last night. love in
    an anger came
And brought a rod, so whipt me with
    the same;
Myrtle the twigs were, merely to
    imply
Love strikes, but 'tis with gentle
    cruelty.
Patient I was: love pitiful grew then
And strok'd the stripes, and I was
    whole again.
Thus, like a bee, love gentle still doth
    bring
Honey to salve where he before did
    sting.

ON HIMSELF

YOUNG I was, but now am old,
    But I am not yet grown cold;

14

I can play, and I can twine
'Bout a virgin like a vine:
In her lap too I can lie
Melting, and in fancy die;
And return to life if she
Claps my cheek, or kisseth me:
Thus, and thus it now appears
That our love outlasts our years.

LOVE'S PLAY AT PUSH-PIN

LOVE and myself, believe me, on a
    day
At childish push-pin, for our sport,
    did play;
I put, he pushed, and, heedless of my
    skin,
Love pricked my finger with a golden
    pin;

15

Since which it festers so that I can
    prove
'Twas but a trick to poison me with
    love:
Little the wound was, greater was the
    smart,
The finger bled, but burnt was all my
    heart.

THE ROSARY

ONE ask'd me where the roses grew.
    I bade him not go seek,
But forthwith bade my Julia show
    A bud in either cheek.

CHERRY-RIPE

CHERRY-RIPE, ripe, ripe, I cry,
    Full and fair ones; come and
    buy.

16

If so be you ask me where
They do grow, I answer: There,
Where my Julia's lips do smile;
There's the land, or cherry-isle,
Whose plantations fully show
All the year where cherries grow.

UPON JULIA'S VOICE

SO smooth, so sweet, so silv'ry is
thy voice
As, could they hear, the damn'd would
make no noise,
But listen to thee, walking in thy
chamber,
Melting melodious words to lutes of
amber.

17

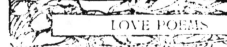
AGAIN

WHEN I thy singing next shall
  hear,
I'll wish I might turn all to ear,
To drink in notes and numbers such
As blessed souls can't hear too much;
Then melted down, there let me lie
Entranc'd and lost confusedly,
And by thy music stricken mute,
Die and be turn'd into a lute.

OF LOVE.   A SONNET

HOW love came in I do not know,
  Whether by the eye, or ear, or
    no;
Or whether with the soul it came
(At first) infused with the same;

18

Whether in part 'tis here or there,
Or, like the soul, whole everywhere,
This troubles me: but I as well
As any other this can tell:
That when from hence she does depart
The outlet then is from the heart.

THE ROCK OF RUBIES, AND THE QUARRY OF PEARLS

SOME ask'd me where the rubies
　grew,
　And nothing I did say:
But with my finger pointed to
　The lips of Julia.
Some ask'd how pearls did grow, and
　where;
　Then spoke I to my girl,

19

To part her lips, and show'd them
   there
The quarrelets of Pearl.

UPON ROSES

UNDER a lawn, than skies more
   clear,
Some ruffled roses nestling were:
And, snugging there, they seem'd to
   lie
As in a flowery nunnery:
They blush'd, and look'd more fresh
   than flowers
Quicken'd of late by pearly showers,
And all because they were possess'd
But of the heat of Julia's breast:
Which, as a warm and moisten'd
   spring,
Gave them their ever-flourishing.

20

THE CHEAT OF CUPID;
OR, THE UNGENTLE
GUEST

ONE silent night of late,
    When every creature rested,
Came one unto my gate
    And, knocking, me molested.

Who's that, said I, beats there,
    And troubles thus the sleepy?
Cast off, said he, all fear,
    And let not locks thus keep ye.

For I a boy am, who
    By moonless nights have swerved;
And all with show'rs wet through,
    And e'en with cold half starved.

21

I pitiful arose,
  And soon a taper lighted;
And did myself disclose
  Unto the lad benighted.

I saw he had a bow
  And wings, too, which did shiver;
And, looking down below,
  I spied he had a quiver.

I to my chimney's shine
  Brought him, as love professes,
And chafed his hands with mine,
  And dried his drooping tresses.

But when he felt him warm'd:
  Let's try this bow of ours,
And string, if they be harm'd,
  Said he, with these late showers.

Forthwith his bow he bent,
  And wedded string and arrow,

22

And struck me, that it went
  Quite through my heart and mar-
    row.

Then, laughing loud, he flew
  Away, and thus said, flying:
Adieu, mine host, adieu,
  I'll leave thy heart a-dying.

DELIGHT IN DISORDER

A SWEET disorder in the dress
    Kindles in clothes a wantonness:
A lawn about the shoulders thrown
Into a fine distraction:
An erring lace which here and there
Enthrals the crimson stomacher:
A cuff neglectful, and thereby
Ribbons to flow confusedly:
A winning wave, deserving note,
In the tempestuous petticoat:

23

A careless shoe-string, in whose tie
I see a wild civility :
Do more bewitch me than when art
Is too precise in every part.

KISSING USURY

Bianca, let
    Me pay the debt
I owe thee for a kiss
    Thou lent'st to me,
    And I to thee
Will render ten for this.

    If thou wilt say
    Ten will not pay
For that so rich a one ;
    I'll clear the sum,
    If it will come
Unto a million.

24

By this, I guess,
Of happiness
Who has a little measure,
  He must of right
  To th' utmost mite
Make payment of his pleasure.

TO JULIA

HOW rich and pleasing thou, my
    Julia, art
In each thy dainty and peculiar part!
First, for thy queenship, on thy head
    is set
Of flowers a sweet commingled coro-
    net:
About thy neck a carcanet is bound,
Made of the ruby, pearl and diamond:
A golden ring that shines upon thy
    thumb:
About thy wrist, the rich dardanium.

C   25

Between thy breasts (than down of
    swans more white)
There plays the sapphire with the
    chrysolite.
No part besides must of thyself be
    known,
But by the topaz, opal, chalcedon.

ZEAL REQUIRED IN LOVE

I'LL do my best to win whene'er I
    woo:
That man loves not who is not zealous
    too.

TO DIANEME

DEAR, though to part it be a hell,
    Yet, Dianeme, now farewell:
Thy frown last night did bid me go,
But whither only grief does know.

26

I do beseech thee ere we part,
If merciful as fair thou art,
Or else desir'st that maids should tell
Thy pity by love's chronicle,
O Dianeme, rather kill
Me, than to make me languish still!
'Tis cruelty in thee to th' height
Thus, thus to wound, not kill out-
    right;
Yet there's a way found, if you please,
By sudden death to give me ease;
And thus devis'd, do thou but this—
Bequeath to me one parting kiss,
So sup'rabundant joy shall be
The executioner of me.

THE FROZEN ZONE; OR, JULIA DISDAINFUL

WHITHER? say, whither shall I
    fly,
To slack these flames wherein I fry?

To the treasures, shall I go,
Of the rain, frost, hail, and snow?
Shall I search the underground,
Where all damps and mists are found?
Shall I seek (for speedy ease)
All the floods and frozen seas?
Or descend into the deep,
Where eternal cold does keep?
These may cool; but there's a zone
Colder yet than anyone:
That's my Julia's breast, where dwells
Such destructive icicles,
As that the congelation will
Me sooner starve than those can kill.

TO MYRRHA, HARD-HEARTED

FOLD now thine arms and hang
the head,
Like to a lily withered;

28

Next look thou like a sickly moon,
Or like Jocasta in a swoon.
Then weep and sigh and softly go,
Like to a widow drown'd in woe,
Or like a virgin full of ruth
For the lost sweetheart of her youth;
And all because, fair maid, thou art
Insensible of all my smart,
And of those evil days that be
Now posting on to punish thee.
The gods are easy, and condemn
All such as are not soft like them.

LOVE ME LITTLE, LOVE ME LONG

YOU say, to me-wards your affection's strong;
Pray love me little, so you love me
long.

Slowly goes far: the mean is best:
  desire,
Grown violent, does either die or tire.

UPON A VIRGIN KISSING
A ROSE

’TWAS but a single rose,
    Till you on it did breathe;
But since, methinks, it shows
    Not so much rose as wreath.

TEARS ARE TONGUES

WHEN Julia chid I stood as mute
    the while
As is the fish or tongueless crocodile.
Air coin’d to words my Julia could
    not hear,

30.

But she could see each eye to stamp a
    tear ;
By which mine angry mistress might
    descry
Tears are the noble language of the
    eye.
And when true love of words is
    destitute
The eyes by tears speak, while the
    tongue is mute.

HIS PROTESTATION TO
PERILLA

NOONDAY and midnight shall at
    once be seen :
Trees, at one time, shall be both sere
    and green :
Fire and water shall together lie
In one self-sweet-conspiring sym-
    pathy :

31

Summer and winter shall at one time
    show
Ripe ears of corn, and up to th' ears
    in snow:
Seas shall be sandless; fields devoid of
    grass;
Shapeless the world, as when all chaos
    was,
Before, my dear Perilla, I will be
False to my vow, or fall away from
    thee.

TO JULIA

PERMIT me, Julia, now to go
    away;
Or by thy love decree me here to stay.
If thou wilt say that I shall live with
    thee,
Here shall my endless tabernacle be:

If not (as banish'd), I will live alone
There where no language ever yet
was known.

ON HIMSELF

LOVE-SICK I am, and must endure
    A desperate grief, that finds no
        cure.
Ah me! I try; and trying, prove
No herbs have power to cure love.
Only one sovereign salve I know,
And that is death, the end of woe.

THE CRUEL MAID

AND cruel maid, because I see
    You scornful of my love and me,
I'll trouble you no more; but go
My way where you shall never know.

33

What is become of me: there I
Will find me out a path to die,
Or learn some way how to forget
You and your name for ever: yet,
Ere I go hence, know this from me,
What will, in time, your fortune be:
This to your coyness I will tell,
And, having spoke it once, farewell.
The lily will not long endure,
Nor the snow continue pure;
The rose, the violet, one day
See both these lady-flowers decay:
And you must fade as well as they.
And it may chance that love may turn,
And, like to mine, make your heart
    burn
And weep to see't; yet this thing do,
That my last vow commends to you:
When you shall see that I am dead,
For pity let a tear be shed;
And, with your mantle o'er me cast,
Give my cold lips a kiss at last:

34

If twice you kiss you need not fear
That I shall stir or live more here.
Next, hollow out a tomb to cover
Me—me, the most despised lover,
And write thereon : *This, reader, know :
Love kill'd this man.*   No more, but so.

TO DIANEME

SWEET, be not proud of those two
   eyes
Which, starlike, sparkle in their skies;
Nor be you proud that you can see
All hearts your captives, yours yet
   free ;
Be you not proud of that rich hair
Which wantons with the love-sick air;
Whenas that ruby which you wear,
Sunk from the tip of your soft ear,
Will last to be a precious stone
When all your world of beauty's gone.

35

HIS MISERY IN A
MISTRESS

WATER, water I espy;
    Come and cool ye all who fry
In your loves; but none as I.

Though a thousand showers be
Still a-falling, yet I see
Not one drop to light on me.

Happy you who can have seas
For to quench ye, or some ease
From your kinder mistresses.

I have one, and she alone,
Of a thousand thousand known,
Dead to all compassion.

Such an one as will repeat
Both the cause and make the heat
More by provocation great.

36

Gentle friends, though I despair
Of my cure, do you beware
Of those girls which cruel are.

UPON A BLACK TWIST ROUNDING THE ARM OF THE COUNTESS OF CARLISLE

I SAW about her spotless wrist,
  Of blackest silk, a curious twist;
Which, circumvolving gently, there
Enthrall'd her arm as prisoner.
Dark was the jail, but as if light
Had met t'engender with the night;
Or so as darkness made a stay
To show at once both night and day.
One fancy more! but if there be
Such freedom in captivity,
I beg to love that ever I
May in like chains of darkness lie.

A RING PRESENTED TO JULIA

JULIA, I bring
        To thee this ring,
Made for thy finger fit;
    To show by this
    That our love is
(Or should be) like to it.

    Close though it be
    The joint is free;
So, when love's yoke is on,
    It must not gall,
    Or fret at all
With hard oppression

    But it must play
    Still either way,
And be, too, such a yoke

As not too wide
To overslide,
Or be so straight to choke.

So we who bear
This beam must rear
Ourselves to such a height
As that the stay
Of either may
Create the burden light.

And as this round
Is nowhere found
To flaw, or else to sever:
So let our love
As endless prove,
And pure as gold for ever.

JULIA'S PETTICOAT

THY azure robe I did behold
As airy as the leaves of gold,

39

Which, erring here, and wandering
   · there,
Pleas'd with transgression ev'rywhere:
Sometimes 'twould pant, and sigh,
   and heave,
As if to stir it scarce had leave:
But, having got it, thereupon
'Twould make a brave expansion.
And pounc'd with stars it showed to
   me
Like a celestial canopy.
Sometimes 'twould blaze, and then
   abate,
Like to a flame grown moderate:
Sometimes away 'twould wildly fling,
Then to thy thighs so closely cling
That some conceit did melt me
   down
As lovers fall into a swoon:
And, all confus'd, I there did lie
Drown'd in delights, but could not
   die.

That leading cloud I follow'd still,
Hoping t'have seen of it my fill;
But ah! I could not: should it move
To life eternal, I could love.

ON JULIA'S BREATH

BREATHE, Julia, breathe, and I'll protest,
Nay more, I'll deeply swear,
That all the spices of the east
Are circumfused there.

ON GILLY-FLOWERS
BEGOTTEN

WHAT was't that fell but now
From that warm kiss of ours?
Look, look! by love I vow
They were two gilly-flowers.

Let's kiss and kiss again,
  For if so be our closes
Make gilly-flowers, then
  I'm sure they'll fashion roses.

LIPS TONGUELESS

FOR my part, I never care
  For those lips that tongue-tied
    are :
Tell-tales I would have them be
Of my mistress and of me.
Let them prattle how that I
Sometimes freeze and sometimes fry :
Let them tell how she doth move
Fore or backward in her love :
Let them speak by gentle tones,
One and th' other's passions :
How we watch, and seldom sleep ;
How by willows we do weep ;

42

How by stealth we meet, and then
Kiss, and sigh, so part again.
This the lips we will permit
For to tell, not publish it.

TO CARNATIONS. A SONG

STAY while ye will, or go
    And leave no scent behind ye :
Yet, trust me, I shall know
    The place where I may find ye.

Within my Lucia's cheek,
    Whose livery ye wear,
Play ye at hide or seek,
    I'm sure to find ye there.

43

TO THE VIRGINS, TO
MAKE MUCH OF TIME

GATHER ye rosebuds while ye may,
    Old time is still a-flying :
And this same flower that smiles to-
    day
    To-morrow will be dying.

The glorious lamp of heaven, the sun,
    The higher he's a-getting,
The sooner will his race be run,
    And nearer he's to setting.

That age is best which is the first,
    When youth and blood are warmer;
But being spent, the worse, and worst
    Times still succeed the former.

44

Then be not coy, but use your time,
  And while ye may go marry:
For having lost but once your prime
  You may for ever tarry.

TO THE LARK

GOOD speed, for I this day
  Betimes my matins say:
Because I do
Begin to woo,
Sweet-singing lark,
Be thou the clerk,
And know thy when
To say, Amen.
And if I prove
Bless'd in my love,
Then thou shalt be
High-priest to me,
At my return,
To incense burn;

45

And so to solemnise
Love's and my sacrifice.

THE BLEEDING HAND; OR, THE SPRIG OF EGLANTINE GIVEN TO A MAID

FROM this bleeding hand of mine
    Take this sprig of eglantine,
Which, though sweet unto your smell,
Yet the fretful briar will tell,
He who plucks the sweets shall prove
Many thorns to be in love.

TO THE ROSE. A SONG

GO, happy rose, and interwove
    With other flowers, bind my
        love.

46

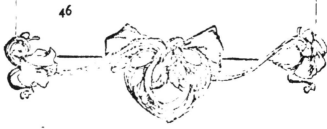

Tell her, too, she must not be
Longer flowing, longer free,
That so oft has fetter'd me.

Say, if she's fretful, I have bands
Of pearl and gold to bind her hands
Tell her, if she struggle still,
I have myrtle rods (at will)
For to tame, though not to kill.

Take thou my blessing thus, and go
And tell her this, but do not so,
Lest a handsome anger fly
Like a lightning from her eye,
And burn thee up as well as I.

HIS RECANTATION

LOVE, I recant,
    And pardon crave
That lately I offended ;

But 'twas,
Alas !
To make a brave,
But no disdain intended.

No more I'll vaunt,
For now I see
Thou only hast the power
To find
And bind
A heart that's free,
And slave it in an hour.

UPON HER VOICE

LET but thy voice engender with
the string,
And angels will be born while thou
dost sing.

48

TO THE WESTERN WIND

SWEET western wind, whose luck
    it is,
  Made rival with the air,
To give Perenna's lip a kiss,
  And fan her wanton hair.

Bring me but one, I'll promise thee,
  Instead of common showers,
Thy wings shall be embalm'd by me,
  And all beset with flowers.

HOW ROSES CAME RED

ROSES at first were white,
    Till they could not agree,
Whether my Sappho's breast
  Or they more white should be

E

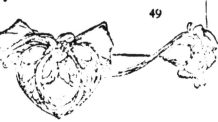

49

But, being vanquish'd quite,
  A blush their cheeks bespread;
Since which, believe the rest,
  The roses first came red.

HOW VIOLETS BECAME BLUE

L OVE on a day, wise poets tell,
    Some time in wrangling spent,
Whether the violets should excel,
  Or she, in sweetest scent.

But Venus having lost the day,
  Poor girls, she fell on you:
And beat ye so, as some dare say,
  Her blows did make ye blue.

TO THE WILLOW-TREE

THOU art to all lost love the
   best,
  The only true plant found,
Wherewith young men and maids dis-
   tress'd,
  And left of love, are crown'd.

When once the lovers' rose is dead,
  Or laid aside forlorn :
Then willow-garlands 'bout the head
  Bedew'd with tears are worn.

When with neglect, the lovers' bane,
  Poor maids rewarded be,
For their love lost, their only gain
  Is but a wreath from thee.

51

And underneath thy cooling shade,
  When weary of the light,
The love-spent youth and love-sick
    maid
  Come to weep out the night.

MRS ELIZ. WHEELER, UNDER THE NAME OF THE LOST SHEP- HERDESS

AMONG the myrtles as I walk'd,
    Love and my sighs thus inter-
      talk'd :
Tell me, said I, in deep distress,
Where I may find my shepherdess.
Thou fool, said love, know'st thou
    not this?
In everything that's sweet she is.

52

In yond' carnation go and seek,
There thou shalt find her lip and cheek:
In that enamell'd pansy by,
There thou shalt have her curious eye:
In bloom of peach and rose's bud,
There waves the streamer of her blood.
'Tis true, said I, and thereupon
I went to pluck them one by one,
To make of parts a union :
But on a sudden all were gone.
At which I stopp'd ; said love, these be
The true resemblances of thee;
For, as these flowers, thy joys must
    die,
And in the turning of an eye :
And all thy hopes of her must wither,
Like those short sweets, ere knit to-
    gether.

TO ANTHEA, WHO MAY COMMAND HIM ANY-THING

BID me to live, and I will live
   Thy Protestant to be,
Or bid me love, and I will give
   A loving heart to thee.

A heart as soft, a heart as kind,
   A heart as sound and free
As in the whole world thou canst find,
   That heart I'll give to thee.

Bid that heart stay, and it will stay
   To honour thy decree :
Or bid it languish quite away,
   And't shall do so for thee.

54

Bid me to weep, and I will weep
   While I have eyes to see:
And, having none, yet I will keep
   A heart to weep for thee.

Bid me despair, and I'll despair
   Under that cypress-tree:
Or bid me die, and I will dare
   E'en death to die for thee.

Thou art my life, my love, my heart,
   The very eyes of me:
And hast command of every part
   To live and die for thee.

I CALL AND I CALL

I CALL, I call: who do ye call?
   The maids to catch this cowslip
      ball:
But since these cowslips fading be,

55

Troth, leave the flowers and, maids,
    take me.
Yet, if that neither you will do,
Speak but the word and I'll take you.

THE BRACELET TO
JULIA

WHY I tie about thy wrist,
    Julia, this my silken twist;
    For what other reason is't,
But to show thee how, in part,
Thou my pretty captive art?
But thy bondslave is my heart;
'Tis but silk that bindeth thee,
Knap the thread and thou art free:
But 'tis otherwise with me;
I am bound, and fast bound, so
That from thee I cannot go;
If I could, I would not so.

56

HIS EMBALMING TO JULIA

FOR my embalming, Julia, do but
    this;
Give thou my lips but their supremest
    kiss,
Or else transfuse thy breath into the
    chest
Where my small relics must for ever
    rest;
That breath the balm, the myrrh, the
    nard shall be,
To give an incorruption unto me.

THE KISS. A DIALOGUE

1. AMONG thy fancies tell me
    this,
   What is the thing we call a kiss?
2. I shall resolve ye what it is.

57

It is a creature born and bred
Between the lips (all cherry-
red),
By love and warm desires fed.
Chor. And makes more soft the bridal
bed.

2. It is an active flame that flies,
First, to the babies of the eyes;
And charms them there with
lullabies.
Chor. And stills the bride, too, when
she cries.

2. Then to the chin, the cheek,
the ear,
It frisks and flies, now here,
now there,
'Tis now far off, and then 'tis
near.
Chor. And here and there and everywhere.

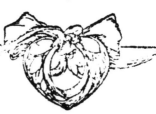

1. Has it a speaking virtue? 2. Yes.
1. How speaks it, say? 2. Do
    you but this ;
    Part your joined lips, then
    speaks your kiss
Chor. And this love's sweetest lan-
    guage is.

1. Has it a body? 2. Aye, and
    wings
    With thousand rare encolour-
    ings ;
    And, as it flies, it gently sings,
Chor. Love honey yields, but never
    stings.

A SHORT HYMN TO VENUS

GODDESS, I do love a girl,
    Ruby-lipp'd and tooth'd with
    pearl ;

59

If so be I may but prove
Lucky in this maid I love,
I will promise there shall be
Myrtles offer'd up to thee.

UPON A DELAYING LADY

COME, come away,
　　Or let me go ;
Must I here stay
Because you're slow,
And will continue so ?
Troth, lady, no.

I scorn to be
A slave to state :
And, since I'm free,
I will not wait
Henceforth at such a rate
For needy fate.

60

If you desire
My spark should glow,
The peeping fire
You must blow,
Or I shall quickly grow
To frost or snow.

UPON HIS JULIA

WILL ye hear what I can say
    Briefly of my Julia?
Black and rolling is her eye,
Double-chinn'd and forehead high;
Lips she has all ruby-red,
Cheeks like cream enclareted;
And a nose that is the grace
And proscenium of her face.
So that we may guess by these
The other parts will richly please.

A HYMN TO VENUS AND CUPID

SEA-BORN goddess, let me be
    By thy son thus grac'd and thee ;
That whene'er I woo, I find
Virgins coy but not unkind.
Let me when I kiss a maid
Taste her lips so overlaid
With love's syrup, that I may,
In your temple when I pray,
Kiss the altar and confess
There's in love no bitterness.

ON JULIA'S PICTURE

HOW am I ravish'd! when I do but
    see
The painter's art in thy sciography?
If so, how much more shall I dote
    thereon
When once he gives it incarnation?

62

UPON SAPPHO SWEET-LY PLAYING AND SWEETLY SINGING

WHEN thou dost play and sweetly
    sing—
Whether it be the voice or string
Or both of them that do agree
Thus to entrance and ravish me—
This, this I know, I'm oft struck mute,
And die away upon thy lute.

HOW PANSIES OR HEART'S-EASE CAME FIRST

FROLIC virgins once these were,
    Over-loving, living here;
Being here their ends denied,
Ran for sweethearts mad, and died.

63

Love, in pity of their tears,
And their loss in blooming years,
For their restless here-spent hours,
Gave them heart's-ease turn'd to
   flowers.

CLOTHES DO BUT CHEAT AND COZEN US

AWAY with silks, away with lawn,
   I'll have no scenes or curtains
    drawn ;
Give me my mistress as she is,
Dress'd in her nak'd simplicities ;
For as my heart e'en so mine eye
Is won with flesh, not drapery.

UPON ELECTRA

WHEN out of bed my love doth
    spring,
'Tis but as day a-kindling;
But when she's up and fully dress'd,
'Tis then broad day throughout the
    east.

TO SPRINGS AND FOUNTAINS

I HEARD ye could cool heat, and
    came
With hope you would allay the same;
Thrice I have wash'd but feel no cold,
Nor find that true which was foretold.
Methinks, like mine, your pulses beat
And labour with unequal heat;
Cure, cure yourselves, for I descry
Ye boil with love as well as I.

65

UPON JULIA'S UNLAC-
ING HERSELF

TELL if thou canst, and truly, whence doth come
This camphor, storax, spikenard, galbanum ;
These musks, these ambers, and those other smells
(Sweet as the vestry of the oracles).
I'll tell thee: while my Julia did unlace
Her silken bodice but a breathing space,
The passive air such odour then assum'd,
As when to Jove great Juno goes perfum'd,
Whose pure immortal body doth transmit
A scent that fills both heaven and earth with it.

66

THE LAWN

WOULD I see lawn, clear as the
    heaven, and thin?
It should be only in my Julia's skin,
Which so betrays her blood as we
    discover
The blush of cherries when a lawn's
    cast over.

TO SYCAMORES

I'M sick of love, O let me lie
    Under your shades to sleep or
    die!
Either is welcome, so I have
Or here my bed, or here my grave.
Why do you sigh, and sob, and keep
Time with the tears that I do weep?

67

Say, have ye sense, or do you prove
What crucifixions are in love?
I know ye do, and that's the why
You sigh for love as well as I.

THE WILLOW GARLAND

A WILLOW garland thou did'st send
  Perfum'd, last day, to me,
Which did but only this portend—
  I was forsook by thee.

Since so it is, I'll tell thee what,
  To-morrow thou shalt see
Me wear the willow, after that
  To die upon the tree.

As beasts unto the altars go
  With garlands dress'd, so I
Will, with my willow-wreath, also
  Come forth and sweetly die.

68

TO THE LITTLE SPINNERS

YE pretty housewives, would ye
  know
The work that I would put ye to?
This, this it should be: for to spin
A lawn for me, so fine and thin
As it might serve me for my skin.
For cruel love has me so whipp'd
That of my skin I all am stripp'd;
And shall despair that any art
Can ease the rawness or the smart,
Unless you skin again each part.
Which mercy if you will but do,
I call all maids to witness to
What here I promise: that no broom
Shall now or ever after come
To wrong a spinner or her loom.

69

TO OENONE

WHAT, conscience, say is it in
    thee,
  When I a heart had one,
To take away that heart from me,
  And to retain thy own?

For shame or pity now incline
  To play a loving part;
Either to send me kindly thine,
  Or give me back my heart.

Covet not both; but if thou dost
  Resolve to part with neither,
Why! yet to show that thou art just,
  Take me and mine together.

70

UPON LOVE

LOVE, I have broke
      Thy yoke,
The neck is free ;
But when I'm next
      Love-vexed,
Then shackle me.

'Tis better yet
      To fret
The feet or hands,
Than to enthral
      Or gall
The neck with bands.

71

THE JIMMALL RING OR TRUE LOVE-KNOT

THOU sent'st to me a true love-
    knot, but I
Returned a ring of jimmals to imply
Thy love had one knot, mine a triple
    tie.

TO PERENNA

HOW long, Perenna, wilt thou see
    Me languish for the love of
    thee?
Consent and play a friendly part
To save, when thou may'st kill a
    heart.

HOW SPRINGS CAME FIRST

THESE springs were maidens once
    that lov'd,
But lost to that they most approv'd:
My story tells by love they were
Turn'd to these springs which we see
    here ;
The pretty whimpering that they
    make,
When of the banks their leave they
    take,
Tells ye but this, they are the same,
In nothing chang'd but in their name.

UPON JULIA

HOW can I choose but love and
    follow her
Whose shadow smells like milder
    pomander?
How can I choose but kiss her, whence
    does come
The storax, spikenard, myrrh, and
    laudanum?

A CAUTION

THAT love last long, let it thy first
    care be
To find a wife that is most fit for thee.
Be she too wealthy or too poor, be
    sure
Love in extremes can never long en-
    dure.

TO THE WATER NYMPHS DRINKING AT THE FOUNTAIN

R EACH, with your whiter hands, to me
  Some crystal of the spring ;
And I about the cup shall see
  Fresh lilies flourishing.

Or else, sweet nymphs, do you but this,
  To th' glass your lips incline ;
And I shall see by that one kiss
  The water turn'd to wine.

75

TO MISTRESS DOROTHY PARSONS

IF thou ask me, dear, wherefore
   I do write of thee no more,
I must answer, sweet, thy part
Less is here than in my heart.

UPON LOVE

I HELD love's head while it did
   ache ;
But so it chanc'd to be,
The cruel pain did his forsake,
   And forthwith came to me.

Ah, me! how shall my grief be still'd?
   Or where else shall we find
One like to me, who must be kill'd
   For being too-too kind?

76

TO PHYLLIS, TO LOVE
AND LIVE WITH HIM

LIVE, live with me, and thou shalt
　　see
The pleasures I'll prepare for thee ;
What sweets the country can afford
Shall bless thy bed and bless thy board.
The soft, sweet moss shall be thy bed
With crawling woodbine over-spread;
By which the silver-shedding streams
Shall gently melt thee into dreams.
Thy clothing, next, shall be a gown
Made of the fleece's purest down.
The tongues of kids shall be thy meat,
Their milk thy drink ; and thou shalt
　　eat
The paste of filberts for thy bread
With cream of cowslips buttered ;
Thy feasting-tables shall be hills
With daisies spread and daffodils,

77

Where thou shalt sit, and red-breast
    by,
For meat, shall give thee melody.
I'll give thee chains and carcanets
Of primroses and violets.
A bag and bottle thou shalt have,
That richly wrought, and this as
    brave;
So that as either shall express
The wearer's no mean shepherdess
At shearing-times, and yearly wakes,
When Themilis his pastime makes,
There thou shalt be; and be the
    wit,
Nay, more, the feast, and grace of it.
On holidays, when virgins meet
To dance the heyes with nimble feet,
Thou shalt come forth, and then
    appear
The queen of roses for that year;
And having danced, 'bove all the best,
Carry the garland from the rest.

In wicker baskets maids shall bring
To thee, my dearest shepherling,
The blushing apple, bashful pear,
And shame-fac'd plum, all simp'ring
    there.
Walk in the groves, and thou shalt find
The name of Phyllis in the rind
Of every straight and smooth-skin tree;
Where kissing that, I'll twice kiss thee.
To thee a sheep-hook I will send,
Be-prank'd with ribands to this end;
This, this alluring hook might be
Less for to catch a sheep than me.
Thou shalt have possets, wassails fine,
Not made of ale, but spiced wine,
To make thy maids and self free mirth,
All sitting near the glitt'ring hearth.
Thou shalt have ribands, roses, rings,
Gloves, garters, stockings, shoes, and
    strings
Of winning colours, that shall move
Others to lust, but me to love.

79

These, nay, and more, thine own shall
    be
If thou wilt love, and live with me.

UPON HIS GREY HAIRS

FLY me not, though I be grey :
    Lady, this I know you'll say ;
Better look the roses red
When with white commingled.
Black your hairs are, mine are white ;
This begets the more delight,
When things meet most opposite.
As in pictures we descry
Venus standing Vulcan by.

TO DIANEME

GIVE me one kiss
    And no more :
If, so be, this
    Makes you poor

To enrich you,
I'll restore
For that one two
Thousand score.

UPON LOVE

I PLAYED with Love, as with the
fire
The wanton Satyr did ;
Nor did I know, or could descry
What under there was hid.

That Satyr he but burnt his lips ;
But mine's the greater smart,
For kissing Love's dissembling chips
The fire scorch'd my heart.

UPON IRENE

A NGRY if Irene be
    But a minute's life with me:
Such a fire I espy
Walking in and out her eye,
As at once I freeze and fry.

LOVE LIGHTLY PLEASED

L ET fair or foul my mistress be,
    Or low, or tall, she pleaseth
      me ;
Or let her walk, or stand, or sit,
The posture hers, I'm pleas'd with it ;
Or let her tongue be still, or stir,
Graceful is every thing from her ;
Or let her grant, or else deny,
My love will fit each history.

82

THE PRIMROSE

ASK me why I send you here
This sweet Infanta of the
year?
Ask me why I send to you
This primrose, thus bepearl'd with
dew?
I will whisper to your ears :
The sweets of love are mix'd with
tears.

Ask me why this flower does show
So yellow-green, and sickly too?
Ask me why the stalk is weak
And bending (yet it doth not break)?
I will answer : These discover
What fainting hopes are in a lover.

83

NO LUCK IN LOVE

I DO love I know not what,
  Sometimes this and sometimes
    that;
All conditions I aim at.

But, as luckless, I have yet
Many shrewd disasters met
To gain her whom I would get.

Therefore now I'll love no more
As I've doted heretofore:
He who must be, shall be poor.

THE HEADACHE

M Y head doth ache,
  O Sappho! take
    Thy fillet,

84

And bind the pain,
Or bring some bane
    To kill it.

But less that part
Than my poor heart
    Now is sick ;
One kiss from thee
Will counsel be
    And physic.

OF LOVE

I'LL get me hence,
    Because no fence
Or fort that I can make here ;
    But love by charms,
    Or else by arms
Will storm, or starving take here.

TO THE MAIDS TO WALK ABROAD

COME, sit we under yonder tree,
　　Where merry as the maids we'll
　be ;
And as on primroses we sit,
We'll venture, if we can, at wit :
If not, at draw-gloves we will play ;
So spend some minutes of the day :
Or else spin out the thread of sands,
Playing at questions and commands :
Or tell what strange tricks love can
　　do,
By quickly making one of two.
Thus we will sit and talk, but tell
No cruel truths of Philomel,
Or Phyllis, whom hard fate forc'd on
To kill herself for Demophon.

But fables we'll relate : how Jove
Put on all shapes to get a love ;
As now a satyr, then a swan ;
A bull but then, and now a man.
Next we will act how young men
    woo,
And sigh, and kiss as lovers do ;
And talk of brides, and who shall
    make
That wedding-smock, this bridal
    cake,
That dress, this sprig, that leaf, this
    vine,
That smooth and silken columbine.
This done, we'll draw lots who shall
    buy
And gild the bays and rosemary ;
What posies for our wedding rings ;
What gloves we'll give and riband-
    ings :
And smiling at ourselves, decree,
Who then the joining priest shall be.

What short, sweet prayers shall be
    said ;
And how the posset shall be made
With cream of lilies, not of kine,
And maiden's-blush, for spiced wine.
Thus, having talked, we'll next
    commend
A kiss to each, and so we'll end.

THE NIGHT-PIECE, TO JULIA

HER eyes the glow-worm lend
    thee,
The shooting stars attend thee ;
    And the elves also,
    Whose little eyes glow
Like the sparks of fire, befriend thee.

No Will-o'-th'-Wisp mislight thee,
Nor snake or slow-worm bite thee ;

58

But on, on thy way
Not making a stay,
Since ghost there's none to affright
thee.

Let not the dark thee cumber:
What though the moon does slumber?
The stars of the night
Will lend thee their light
Like tapers clear without number.

Then, Julia, let me woo thee,
Thus, thus to come unto me;
And when I shall meet
Thy silv'ry feet
My soul I'll pour into thee.

A KISS

WHAT is a kiss? Why this, as
some approve:
The sure, sweet cement, glue, and
lime of love.

89

UPON LOVE

IN a dream, Love bade me go
   To the galleys there to row;
In the vision I ask'd why?
Love as briefly did reply,
'Twas better there to toil, than prove
The turmoils they endure that love.
   I awoke, and then I knew
   What Love said was too-too
      true;
   Henceforth therefore I will be,
   As from love, from trouble free.
None pities him that's in the snare,
And warn'd before would not beware.

UPON LOVE

A CRYSTAL vial Cupid brought,
   Which had a juice in it;

Of which who drank, he said no
  thought
Of love he should admit.

I, greedy of the prize, did drink,
  And emptied soon the glass;
Which burnt me so, that I do think
  The fire of hell it was.

Give me my earthen cups again,
  The crystal I contemn;
Which, though enchas'd with pearls,
  contain
  A deadly draught in them.

And thou, O Cupid! Come not to
  My threshold, since I see,
For all I have, or else can do,
  Thou still wilt cozen me.

TO SILVIA

I AM holy while I stand
   Circum-crost by thy pure hand;
But when that is gone, again
I, as others, am profane.

TO ELECTRA

I DARE not ask a kiss,
   I dare not beg a smile,
Lest having that, or this,
   I might grow proud the while.

No, no, the utmost share
   Of my desire shall be
Only to kiss that air
   That lately kissed thee.

WHAT KIND OF MIS-TRESS HE WOULD HAVE

BE the mistress of my choice
   Clean in manners, clear in
      voice;
Be she witty, more than wise,
Pure enough, though not precise;
Be she showing in her dress
Like a civil wilderness;
That the curious may detect
Order in a sweet neglect;
Be she rolling in her eye,
Tempting all the passers-by;
And each ringlet of her hair
An enchantment, or a snare
For to catch the lookers-on;
But herself held fast by none.

93

Let her Lucrece all day be,
Thais in the night to me.
Be she such as neither will
Famish me nor overfill.

DENIAL IN WOMEN NO DISHEARTENING TO MEN

WOMEN, although they ne'er so
    goodly make it,
Their fashion is, but to say no, to
    take it.

TO ANTHEA

COME, Anthea, know thou this,
    Love at no time idle is ;
Let's be doing, though we play
But at push-pin half the day ;

94

Chains of sweet bents let us make
Captive one, or both, to take :
In which bondage we will lie,
Souls transfusing thus, and die.

THE RAINBOW, OR CURIOUS COVENANT

MINE eyes, like clouds, were
  drizzling rain ;
And as they thus did entertain
The gentle beams from Julia's sight
To mine eyes levell'd opposite,
O thing admir'd ! there did appear
A curious rainbow smiling there ;
Which was the covenant that she
No more would drown mine eyes or
  me.

95

STOOL-BALL

AT stool-ball, Lucia, let us play
　　For sugar-cakes and wine:
Or for a tansy let us pay,
　　The loss, or thine, or mine.

If thou, my dear, a winner be
　　At trundling of the ball,
The wager thou shalt have, and me,
　　And my misfortunes all.

But if, my sweetest, I shall get,
　　Then I desire but this:
That likewise I may pay the bet
　　And have for all a kiss.

TO SAPPHO

LET us now take time and play,
　　Love, and live here while we
　　may;

96

Drink rich wine, and make good
    cheer,
While we have our being here ;
For once dead and laid i' th' grave,
No return from thence we have.

LOVE PALPABLE

I PRESS'D my Julia's lips, and in
    the kiss
Her soul and love were palpable in
    this.

O ACTION HARD TO
AFFECTION

NOTHING hard or harsh can prove
    Unto those that truly love.

THE BRACELET
OF PEARL: TO SILVIA

I BRAKE thy bracelet 'gainst my
    will,
  And, wretched, I did see
Thee discomposed then, and still
  Art discontent with me.

One gem was lost, and I will get
  A richer pearl for thee,
Than ever, dearest Silvia, yet
  Was drunk to Antony.

Or, for revenge, I'll tell thee what
  Thou for the breach shalt do;
First crack the strings, and after that
  Cleave thou my heart in two.

98

UPON THE ROSES IN JULIA'S BOSOM

THRICE happy roses, so much
    grac'd to have
Within the bosom of my love your
    grave.
Die when ye will, your sepulchre is
    known,
Your grave her bosom is, the lawn
    the stone.

MAIDS' NAYS ARE NOTHING

MAIDS' nays are nothing, they are
    shy
But to desire what they deny.

99

LOVERS: HOW THEY COME AND PART

A GYGES' ring they bear about
    them still,
To be, and not seen when and where
    they will.
They tread on clouds, and though
    they sometimes fall,
They fall like dew, but make no
    noise at all.
So silently they one to th' other
    come,
As colours steal into the pear or
    plum,
And air-like, leave no pression to be
    seen
Where'er they met or parting place
    has been.

IN PRAISE OF WOMEN

O JUPITER, should I speak ill
    Of woman-kind, first die I
      will ;
Since that I know, 'mong all the rest
Of creatures, woman is the best.

TO ELECTRA. LOVE LOOKS FOR LOVE

L OVE love begets, then never be
    Unsoft to him who's smooth to
      thee.
Tigers and bears, I've heard some say,
For proffer'd love will love repay :
None are so harsh, but if they find
Softness in others, will be kind ;
Affection will affection move,
Then you must like because I love.

101

TO OENONE

SWEET Oenone, do but say
   Love thou dost, though love says
      nay.
Speak me fair ; for lovers be
Gently kill'd by flattery.

TO SAPPHO

SAPPHO, I will choose to go
   Where the northern winds do
      blow
Endless ice and endless snow :
Rather than I once would see
But a winter's face in thee,
To benumb my hopes and me.

102

THE MAIDEN-BLUSH

SO look the mornings when the sun
    Paints them with fresh ver-
      milion :
So cherries blush, and Kathern pears,
And apricots in youthful years :
So corals look more lovely red,
And rubies lately polished :
So purest diaper doth shine,
Stain'd by the beams of claret wine :
As Julia looks when she doth dress
Her either cheek with bashfulness.

TO DIANEME

I COULD but see thee yesterday
    Stung by a fretful bee ;
And I the javelin suck'd away,
    And heal'd the wound in thee.

103

A thousand thorns and briars and
  stings,
  I have in my poor breast;
Yet ne'er can see that salve which
  brings
  My passions any rest.

As love shall help me, I admire
  How thou canst sit, and smile
To see me bleed, and not desire
  To staunch the blood the while.

If thou, compos'd of gentle mould,
  Art so unkind to me;
What dismal stories will be told
  Of those that cruel be?

TO OENONE

THOU sayest Love's dart
    Hath pricked thy heart;
And thou dost languish too:

If one poor prick
Can make thee sick,
Say, what would many do?

TO ELECTRA

SHALL I go to Love and tell,
  Thou art all turned icicle?
Shall I say her altars be
Disadorn'd and scorn'd by thee?
O beware! in time submit;
Love has yet no wrathful fit:
If her patience turns to ire,
Love is then consuming fire.

TO MISTRESS AMY POTTER

AH me! I love; give him your
  hand to kiss
Who both your wooer and your poet is.

105

Nature has precompos'd us both to
    love :
Your part's to grant; my scene must
    be to move.
Dear, can you like, and liking love
    your poet ?
If you say "Aye," blush-guiltiness
    will show it.
Mine eyes must woo you, though I
    sigh the while :
True love is tongueless as a crocodile.
And you may find in love these differ-
    ing parts—
Wooers have tongues of ice, but
    burning hearts.

UPON LOVE

LOVE is a circle, and an endless
    sphere ;
From good to good, revolving here
    and there.

UPON LOVE

SOME salve to every sore we may
    apply ;
Only for my wound there's no remedy.
Yet if my Julia kiss me, there will be
A sovereign balm found out to cure me.

WRITING

WHEN words we want, Love
    teacheth to indite ;
And what we blush to speak, she bids
    us write.

UPON LOVE

LOVE brought me to a silent grove
    And show'd me there a tree,
Where some had hang'd themselves
    for love,
    And gave a twist to me.

107

The halter was of silk and gold,
  That he reach'd forth unto me;
No otherwise than if he would
  By dainty things undo me.

He bade me then that necklace use;
  And told me, too, he maketh
A glorious end by such a noose,
  His death for love that taketh.

'Twas but a dream; but had I been
  There really alone,
My desp'rate fears in love had seen
  Mine execution.

TO SAPPHO

THOU say'st thou lov'st me,
    Sappho; I say no;
But would to love I could believe
  'twas so!

108

Pardon my fears, sweet Sappho; I
    desire
That thou be righteous found, and I
    the liar

ON LOVE

LOVE is a kind of war: hence
    those who fear!
No cowards must his royal ensigns
    bear.

ANOTHER

WHERE love begins, there dead
    thy first desire:
A spark neglected makes a mighty
    fire.

A HYMN TO CUPID

THOU, thou that bear'st the sway,
  With whom the sea-nymphs
  play;
And Venus, every way:
When I embrace thy knee,
And make short pray'rs to thee,
In love then prosper me.
This day I go to woo;
Instruct me how to do
This work thou put'st me to.
From shame my face keep free;
From scorn I beg of thee,
Love, to deliver me:
So shall I sing thy praise,
And to thee altars raise,
Unto the end of days.

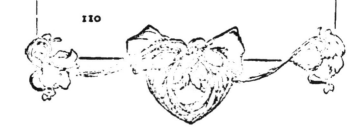

HOW HIS SOUL CAME ENSNARED

MY soul would one day go and seek
    For roses, and in Julia's cheek
A richesse of those sweets she found,
As in another Rosamond.
But gathering roses as she was,
Not knowing what would come to
    pass,
It chanc'd a ringlet of her hair
Caught my poor soul, as in a snare:
Which ever since has been in thrall;
Yet freedom, she enjoys withal.

THE SHOWER OF BLOSSOMS

LOVE in a shower of blossoms came
    Down, and half drown'd me with
    the same:

111

The blooms that fell were white and
    red ;
But with such sweets comminglèd,
As whether, this, I cannot tell
My sight was pleas'd more, or my
    smell :
But true it was, as I roll'd there,
Without a thought of hurt or fear,
Love turn'd himself into a bee,
And with his javelin wounded me :
From which mishap this use I make,
Where most sweets are, there lies a
    snake :
Kisses and favours are sweet things ;
But those have thorns and these have
    stings.

UPON HIMSELF

I LATELY fri'd but now behold
  I freeze as fast, and shake for cold.

And in good faith I'd thought it
    strange
T' have found in me this sudden
    change;
But that I understood by dreams
These only were but Love's extremes;
Who fires with hope the lover's heart,
And starves with cold the self-same
    part.

THE BONDMAN

BIND me but to thee with thine
    hair,
  And quickly I shall be
Made by that fetter or that snare
  A bondman unto thee.

Or if thou tak'st that bond away,
  Then bore me through the ear,
And by the law I ought to stay
  For ever with thee here.

113

TO SILVIA

PARDON my trespass, Silvia; I
    confess
My kiss out-went the bounds of
    shamefastness:
None is discreet at all times; no, not
    Jove
Himself, at one time, can be wise and
    love.

UPON CUPID

LOVE, like a beggar, came to me
    With hose and doublet torn:
His shirt bedangling from his knee,
    With hat and shoes outworn.

He ask'd an alms; I gave him bread,
    And meat too, for his need:

114

Of which, when he had fully fed,
  He wished me all good speed.

Away he went, but as he turn'd
  (In faith I know not how)
He touch'd me so, as that I burn['d],
  And am tormented now.

Love's silent flames and fires obscure
  Then crept into my heart ;
And though I saw no bow, I'm sure
  His finger was the dart.

AN HYMN TO LOVE

I WILL confess
  With cheerfulness,
Love is a thing so likes me,
  That let her lay
  On me all day,
I'll kiss the hand that strikes me

115

I will not, I,
Now blubb'ring, cry,
It, ah! too late repents me,
That I did fall
To love at all,
Since love so much contents me.

No, no, I'll be
In fetters free:
While others they sit wringing
Their hands for pain,
I'll entertain
The wounds of love with singing.

With flowers and wine,
And cakes divine,
To strike me I will tempt thee:
Which done; no more
I'll come before
Thee and thine altars empty.

LOVE IS A SYRUP

LOVE is a syrup ; and whoe'er we
 see
Sick and surcharg'd with this satiety,
Shall by this pleasing trespass quickly
 prove
There's loathsomeness e'en in the
 sweets of love.

LEAVEN

LOVE is a leaven ; and a loving
 kiss
The leaven of a loving sweetheart is.

117

UPON LOVE, BY WAY OF QUESTION AND ANSWER

I BRING ye love:
    Quest. What will love do?
     Ans. Like and dislike ye.
I bring ye love :
    Quest. What will love do?
    Ans. Stroke ye to strike ye.
I bring ye love :
    Quest. What will love do?
    Ans. Love will befool ye.
I bring ye love :
    Quest. What will love do?
    Ans. Heat ye to cool ye.
I bring ye love :
    Quest. What will love do?
    Ans. Love gifts will send ye.

118

I bring ye love:
> *Quest.* What will love do?
> *Ans.* Stock ye to spend ye.

I bring ye love:
> *Quest.* What will love do?
> *Ans.* Love will fulfil ye.

I bring ye love:
> *Quest.* What will love do?
> *Ans.* Kiss ye to kill ye.

THE BEGGAR

SHALL I a daily beggar be,
　　For love's sake asking alms of
　　　　thee?
Still shall I crave, and never get
A hope of my desired bit?

Ah, cruel maids! I'll go my way,
Whereas, perchance, my fortunes may

119

Find out a threshold or a door
That may far sooner speed the poor:
Where thrice we knock, and none
    will hear,
Cold comfort still I'm sure lives there.

A DIALOGUE BETWEEN HIMSELF AND MRS ELIZA WHEELER, UNDER THE NAME OF AMARYLLIS

HER.

MY dearest love, since thou wilt go,
    And leave me here behind thee,
For love or pity let me know
The place where I may find thee

120

AMA.

In country meadows pearl'd with dew,
  And set about with lilies,
There, filling maunds with cowslips,
    you
  May find your Amaryllis.

HER.

What have the meads to do with thee,
  Or with thy youthful hours?
Live thou at Court, where thou
    mayst be
  The queen of men, not flowers.

Let country wenches make 'em fine
  With posies, since 'tis fitter
For thee with richest gems to shine,
  And like the stars to glitter.

AMA.

You set too high a rate upon
  A shepherdess so homely.

L

HER.

Believe it, dearest, there's not one
  I' th' Court that's half so comely.

I prithee stay. *Ama.* I must away;
  Let's kiss first, then we'll sever.

AMBO.

And though we bid adieu to-day,
  We shall not part for ever.

OF LOVE

1. INSTRUCT me now what love
  will do.
2. 'Twill make a tongueless man to
  woo.
1. Inform me next, what love will do.
2. 'Twill strangely make a one of two.

122

1. Teach me besides, what love will
   do.
2. 'Twill quickly mar, and make ye
   too.
1. Tell me now last, what love will
   do.
2. 'Twill hurt and heal a heart pierc'd
   through.

TO PERENNA

THOU say'st I'm dull; if edgeless so
    I be,
I'll whet my lips, and sharpen love on
    thee.

ON HIMSELF

LET me not live if I not love:
    Since I as yet did never prove
Where pleasures met, at last do find
All pleasures meet in womankind.

ANOTHER ON LOVE

LOVE'S of itself too sweet; the
  best of all
Is, when love's honey has a dash of
  gall.

HIS COVENANT; OR, PROTESTATION TO JULIA

WHY dost thou wound and break
  my heart,
As if we should for ever part?
Hast thou not heard an oath from me,
After a day, or two, or three,
I would come back and live with thee?
Take, if thou dost distrust that vow,
This second protestation now.

124

Upon thy cheek that spangled tear,
Which sits as dew of roses there,
That tear shall scarce be dried before
I'll kiss the threshold of thy door.
Then weep not, sweet; but this much
    know,
I'm half return'd before I go.

SONG. HIS MISTRESS TO HIM AT HIS FAREWELL

YOU may vow I'll not forget
    To pay the debt.
Which to thy memory stands as due
    As faith can seal it you;
Take then tribute of my tears,
    So long as I have fears
    To prompt me I shall ever
Languish and look, but thy return
    see never.

125

Oh then to lessen my despair
Print thy lips into the air,
So by this
Means I may kiss thy kiss
Whenas some kind
Wind
Shall hither waft it, and in lieu
My lips shall send a 1000 back to you.

UPON PARTING

Go hence away, and in thy parting
know
'Tis not my voice but Heaven's that
bids thee go;
Spring hence thy faith, nor think it
ill desert
I find in thee that makes me thus to
part
But voice of fame, and voice of Heaven
have thundered

126

We both were lost, if both of us not
    sundered.
Fold now thine arms, and in thy last
    look rear
One sigh of love, and cool it with a
    tear.
Since part we must, let's kiss; that
    done, retire
With as cold frost as erst we met with
    fire;
With such white vows as fate can
    ne'er dissever,
But truth knit fast; and so, farewell
    for ever

TURNBULL AND SPEARS, PRINTERS,
EDINBURGH.

THE LOVER'S LIBRARY

Edited by Frederic Chapman

Uniform with this Volume

Price 1/6 net   CLOTH   Price 50 cents net
Price 2/- net   LEATHER   Price 75 cents net

Vol. I.   THE LOVE POEMS OF SHELLEY
Vol. II.   THE LOVE POEMS OF ROBERT BROWNING
Vol. III. THE SILENCE OF LOVE
Vol. IV.   THE LOVE POEMS OF TENNYSON
Vol. V.   THE LOVE POEMS OF LANDOR
Vol. VI.   THE LOVE POEMS OF E. B. BROWNING
Vol. VII. THE LOVE POEMS OF ROBERT BURNS
Vol. VIII. THE LOVE POEMS OF HERRICK
Vol. IX.   THE LOVE POEMS OF SIR JOHN SUCKLING
Vol. X.   THE LOVE POEMS OF W. S. BLUNT (PROTEUS)
Vol. XI.   THE SONNETS OF SHAKE-SPEARE
Vol. XII. CUPID AND PSYCHE

Other Volumes in Preparation

Flowers of Parnassus

A Series of Famous Poems Illustrated

Each Volume containing from Eight to Twelve
Designs

Under the General Editorship of

F. B. Money-Coutts

Demy 16mo (5½ × 4½), gilt top

Price 1/- net   CLOTH   Price 50 cents net
Price 1/6 net   LEATHER   Price 75 cents net

Vol. I.   Gray's Elegy. *Illustrated.*
Vol. II.   Browning's The Statue and the
            Bust. *Illustrated.*
Vol. III.   Phillips's Marpessa.
Vol. IV.   The Blessed Damozel. By D. G.
            Rossetti. *Illustrated.*
Vol. V.   The Nut-Brown Maid. A New
            Version. *Illustrated.*
Vol. VI.   Tennyson's A Dream of Fair
            Women.
Vol. VII.   Tennyson's The Day-Dream.
Vol. VIII. Suckling's A Ballade upon a
            Wedding. *Illustrated.*
Vol. IX.   Rubáiyát of Omar Khayyám.
Vol. X.   Pope's The Rape of the Lock.
Vol. XI.   Watts-Dunton's Christmas at the
            Mermaid.
Vol. XII.   Blake's Songs of Innocence.
Vol. XIII. Shelley's Sensitive Plant.
Vol. XIV.   Phillips's Christ in Hades.
Vol. XV.   Watson's Wordsworth's Grave.
Vol. XVI.   Reliques of Stratford-on-Avon.
Vol. XVII. Milton's Lycidas.

An Illustrated Prospectus post free.